NORWICH

Volume 1

A Portrait in Old Picture Postcards

by

Philip Standley

Foreword by Michael V. Dixon

S. B. Publications
1988

Dedicated to my wife, Mary; my daughter, Sarah; and my son, Paul.

First published in 1988 by S. B. Publications

5 Queen Margaret's Road, Loggerheads, Nr. Market Drayton, Shropshire, TF9 4EP.

1st Reprint 1988

2nd Reprint 1989

ISBN 1 870708 09 1

Typeset and printed by Geo. R. Reeve Ltd., Wymondham, Norfolk NR18 0BD.

CONTENTS

CONTENTS CONTINUED

CONTENTS CONTINUED

FOREWORD

by

Michael V. Dixon

Founder Chairman of Norfolk Postcard Club

The traveller entering the city of Norwich is met with the sign NORWICH – A FINE CITY and it is with this in mind I look at this miscellany of views of old Norwich. One should remember Norwich has been a fine and prominent city since the day when it was the second city in the land to London; accepting the riches flowing from the wool trade and the wealth created by the influx of 'strangers'; the Jewish community, Flemish weavers and the Huguenot refugees.

The mediaeval city bounded by the river and its gated wall determined the shape of the city and many of its magnificent buildings that remain. Norwich today is a photographer's paradise with panoramic views from Mousehold Heath, quaint corners and alleyways, fine buildings and carpeted throughout with flowers. I have no doubt that photographers found Norwich just as stimulating at the turn of this century and as a result, produced a comprehensive record in picture postcards that were sent with pride by the citizens and visitors alike. They are now avidly collected for the nostalgia they evoke of that most inventive period of English history – in essence a social record.

Having known Philip Standley for many years as a friend and founder member of the Norfolk Postcard Club, I believe his selection of Norwich picture postcards to be second to none, and the postcards featured in this book encapsulate the proud and bustling capital of East Anglia. Having myself been totally absorbed wandering, or rather leafing, through these streets and events in Norwich, I am sure that readers will find equal pleasure as they turn the pages; savouring the past and our heritage which we are duty bound to preserve.

INTRODUCTION

The first pictures on postcards in this country were published in 1894. These early picture cards were known as 'Court Cards', smaller in size than the standard cards of today, and sharing the space of one side with the correspondence. In 1902, the standard size was introduced and new Post Office regulations permitted one side of the postcard to be used for the illustration, and the reverse side for the correspondence and address.

During the early years of this century, millions of postcards were posted annually, encouraged by the cheap ½d postage rate and the vast output and choice of postcards published, depicting every subject imaginable. This era was known as the 'Golden Age of Postcards'.

Postcard collecting became a national craze and almost every household could boast of an album of cards for visitors to see and admire. The usage and collection of postcards remained very popular until the end of World War I, after which it went into a gradual decline, caused mainly by a rise in postage rates and the increased use of the telephone. Many fine collections were to lie dormant for many years and it is only during the last ten years that they have been rediscovered and today postcard collecting is as popular as ever.

Topographical cards are the most sought after by today's collectors. Norfolk cards are no exception and are in great demand, especially the better photographic examples of a collector's home town.

During the 'Golden Age' there were numerous postcard publishers, including Raphael Tuck, Valentines, Judges, W.H. Smith and Jarrolds, who started producing postcards in the late 1890s and are still publishing today. Other local publishers included Pioneer, Fred Fisher and Tom Nokes, all combining to leave a comprehensive record of life in a vibrant provincial city.

Norwich, like most cities, has changed greatly over the last hundred years and is, of course, still changing. One of the best ways to illustrate this transformation is to take a 'snap shot' of life in the city at the turn of the century, as preserved on picture postcards that were so popular at the time.

This book follows a nostalgic tour of Norwich commencing at the Market Place, then following a route to include St. Giles, Earlham Road, Newmarket Road, St. Stephen's Street, the Castle, Prince of Wales Road, Riverside, Magdalen Street, Aylsham Road, Dereham Road, with a few detours to show places of particular interest. A selection of views of surrounding villages, local events, disasters and transport are also included.

A further volume is planned in the near future to feature the city's social history and surrounding villages in greater detail. I am always interested in seeing any postcards of local interest.

I trust that this book brings back many happy memories to readers who remember Norwich as it used to be, to show the younger generation how the city has changed, and to give as much pleasure to readers as I have had in selecting these postcards and writing this book.

Philip Standley
Wymondham
August 1988

THE CITY ARMS OF NORWICH

The City Arms illustrated on a postcard published by Stoddart & Co of Halifax in their 'Ja-Ja' heraldic series, which covered almost every city and town in the British Isles.

The Arms have been used by the city since the 14th century and were later confirmed on a visitation of the heralds in 1562. The official description of the Arms is "Gules, a Castle Domed Argent, in base a lion passant guardant", which means on a red shield there is a domed castle in silver with a golden lion underneath.

MARKET PLACE, c. 1931

A view of Market Place with the old market stalls bordered by the old Municipal Buildings, the Guildhall and the shops lining part of Guildhall Hill. The shops shown were occupied by (from left to right): Chamberlins, drapers and milliners; Ellison, tobacconist; Dean and Palmer, tailors; and Hipps (1931) Ltd., tailors.

Shortly after this picture was taken, the row of buildings, to the left of the Guildhall, were demolished to make way for the War Memorial Gardens and the new City Hall built between 1932 and 1938 and designed by C.H. James and S.R. Pierce.

In the centre foreground, the statue of Wellington erected in 1854 was moved to the Cathedral Close in 1937.

MARKET PLACE, c. 1910

A close-up view of the old market stalls in Market Place with the buildings on Guildhall Hill in the background.
Notice the well-laden flower stalls and the fashions of the day.

3

MARKET PLACE, p.u. 1914

Soldiers of the Essex Regiment assembled in Market Place prior to their departure with the British Expeditionary Force to France in August, 1914.

In the background the buildings include: British Gas Light Co. Ltd. (now Bookmart); St. Peter Mancroft Church; Market Café (now a clothes shop) with many soldiers queuing for refreshments; and the 'Sir Garnet Wolseley' public house.

The barber appears to have been very busy administering the regulation 'short back and sides'.

The Walk and St. Peter Mancroft, Norwich

GENTLEMAN'S WALK AND ST. PETER MANCROFT CHURCH

Looking down Gentleman's Walk before pedestrianisation and showing the altered Market Place with the packed rows of nearly 200 multi-coloured canvas-topped stalls. Norwich Market Place is one of the largest market areas in the country. Notice the Public Shelter sign in the left foreground, the H. Samuel clock, and the buildings to the right of St. Peter Mancroft Church which have been demolished and replaced by the Bethel Street Car Park, next to the Library.
St. Peter Mancroft Church, one of the largest parish churches in the country, was built in Perpendicular style between 1430 and 1455. It is particularly noted for its hammerbeam roof, rich communion plate, and grand peal of twelve bells. The total height of the tower and steeple is 146 feet.

5

HAYMARKET, p.u. 1935

Looking towards the lower end of Haymarket and photographed from the junctions with Brigg Street and Orford Place. In the background is the parish Church of St. Peter Mancroft, 212 feet in length, with no break between chancel and nave to spoil the magnificent sweep from end to end. One of its finest features is the clerestory with its seventeen windows, clearly shown in the centre of the postcard.

On the left are Burton the tailors and the Haymarket Picture House, which was showing 'Change of Heart' at the time. The Haymarket Picture House opened in 1911, enlarged in 1921 and 1929, and following its closure, the building was demolished in 1959.

Notice the Burton's window advertisement for 37/-, the double row of tramlines in the foreground, and the gardens surrounding Sir Thomas Browne's statue, replaced by a paved area in 1972.

THE GUILDHALL, NORWICH

THE GUILDHALL, c. 1912

The Guildhall stands in the north-west corner of Market Place and was built between 1407 and 1413. The exterior was restored after 1861, but the east end with its diamond pattern in flint and freestone is part of the original building. The clock and turret were added in 1850.

The interior of the Guildhall houses the magnificent Council Chamber completed in 1535. It features a fine carved ceiling, linenfold panelling, many portraits and 15th-century stained glass.

The Guildhall was used continuously as the city's administrative centre from 1535 until 1938. It also housed the magnificent collection of City Regalia; this is now kept in the City Hall.

The Guildhall is open to the public and today is used by the Tourist Information Office.

London Street, Norwich

LONDON STREET, c. 1903

London Street has been one of the busiest shopping streets in the city since the nineteenth century. It possesses many exclusive shops and this view looks up London Street towards the Cathedral having been photographed from the corner of Castle Street.

On the left is Bullen's, jewellers, occupying a building on the corner of Swan Lane and built in c. 1840. Next door is John Corder, chemists. On the opposite side of the street the buildings include Coe's, optician and photographer, and the London and Provincial Bank, later Barclays Bank and now occupied by Waterstone's Bookshop.

LONDON STREET, p.u. 1942

An interesting and unusual view of London Street photographed from the upper windows of the building now occupied by Stead & Simpson on the corner of Castle Street.

On the left of the picture, Garland's was destroyed by fire in August, 1970, and Bullen's still occupy the same premises.

In the centre background, the cupola belongs to the National Provincial Bank, now the National Westminster Bank, built in 1924 and designed by F. Palmer and W. Holden.

Notice the two-way traffic; the scene of many traffic jams. London Street has now been pedestrianised and was the precursor of many similar schemes throughout the country.

GUILDHALL CORNER, p.u. 1939

Guildhall Corner photographed at the junction of Guildhall Hill, London Street and Exchange Street.
On the left, the shops occupy the ground level of a former Queen Anne mansion house built in the early eighteenth century.
At the time, the premises were occupied by: Dean & Palmer, tailors; Willerbys, tailors; Princes Café and Restaurant,
formerly the old established Rossi's gold and silversmiths shop which closed in 1936; F. Lambert, tobacconist; and on the
corner with Exchange Street, the Corner Tea House.
On the right, Jarrold's can just be seen. The famous local store was designed by Skipper and built between 1903 and 1905,
with the corner and facade in Exchange Street added later.
Notice the two-way traffic and the policeman on point duty.

Norwich City Fire Station.

NORWICH CITY FIRE STATION, c. 1905

Norwich City Fire Station was situated at 12-14 Pottergate, next to the junction with Lower Goat Lane. It was opened in September, 1898 and later closed in 1934, when it moved to new premises in Bethel Street which were opened in November 1934, by the Lord Mayor.

The postcard, made up from three separate photographs, shows various horse-drawn fire engines and items of equipment. The card was sent to Supt. Bayliss at Manchester Fire Station with the message, 'This is a photo of my station, yours faithfully, Stanley Shaw, Chief Engineer'.

THE HIPPODROME AND THEATRE ROYAL, 1903

A rare postcard showing the Theatre Royal which was renamed The Norwich Hippodrome for one year in 1903.

In 1758, Thomas Ivory built a theatre next to the Assembly House in Theatre Street. It was known as the Concert Hall and licensed as a theatre in 1768. In the early nineteenth century, the theatre was demolished and the new Theatre Royal was opened on 27th March, 1826.

In 1903, the theatre was sold by Fred Morgan to Bostock and Fitt and known as the Hippodrome. One year later, the Grand Opera House in St. Giles Street was bought by Bostock and Fitt, renamed the Hippodrome, and the theatre in Theatre Street reverted back to the Theatre Royal and leased by Fred Morgan.

The Theatre Royal was destroyed by fire on 22nd June, 1934. It was completely rebuilt and reopened on 30th September, 1935.

The Hippodrome in St. Giles' Street became a top variety theatre and music hall. It closed in 1960 and was later demolished to make way for a multi-storey car park.

COW HILL AND WILLOW LANE, c. 1912

Looking up from Pottergate and showing Willow Lane on the left and Cow Hill on the right. The cobbled surfaces were covered over in 1925.

St. Giles' Church was built in the late 14th century and has a splendid perpendicular nave and hammerbeam roof. The porch was added in the 15th century and the chancel in 1866-7. The church tower is 120 feet high and is the tallest of all the city churches. The unusual cupola on top was added in 1737.

Notice the crowstep gable end belonging to the house in the centre of the picture.

ST. GILES' GATES, c. 1906

Looking down Upper St. Giles' Street and photographed at the junction with Earlham Road and Grapes Hill.
Further down, St. Giles' Street has many fine Georgian buildings and during the eighteenth and nineteenth centuries was
the residential area of many celebrated doctors.
On the left can be seen the shops belonging to English, chemists, and Davidson Bros., fruiterers. In the centre, the tram,
number 31, is on the Unthank Road route, and on the right is the St. Giles' Gates Stores public house. This was owned by
Cooper, Brown & Co., brewers of Eaton and East Dereham. It was later demolished to make way for the inner link road.

96, ST. GILES' STREET, c. 1910

A rare and very collectable postcard illustrating the butcher's shop owned by Mr. Sandford, situated at 96, St. Giles' Street.
The owner, staff and delivery boys stand proudly in front of sides of beef and pork.
The local health authorities would not approve of similar displays today!

ST. JOHN THE BAPTIST (R.C.) CHURCH, 1909

The Roman Catholic Church of St. John the Baptist was designed in Early English style by George Gilbert Scott Junior and John Oldrid Scott. It was built on the site of the former Norfolk County Gaol and was paid for by the generosity of the 15th Duke of Norfolk.

Construction commenced in 1884 and completed in 1910, shortly after this photograph was taken. The church is 275 ft long and 81 ft high inside the chancel.

The church was given cathedral status by the Vatican on 13th March, 1976 and the Bishop was enthroned on 2nd June, 1976. Notice the tram shelter in the centre foreground.

EARLHAM ROAD, p.u. 1907

A flock of sheep driven along Earlham Road by a shepherd and his dog. The tram, number 10, waits patiently behind and is close to the junction with Heigham Road. To the right, and immediately behind the tram, is R. Betts, fishmongers.
Animals, not motor cars, caused traffic delays in those days!

EARLHAM ROAD, p.u. 1907

Looking westwards along Earlham Road with Alexandra Road on the right. At the time of this photograph, the house on the right was a private school for young ladies owned by the Misses Boobyer and Callis. Later, it became the Lonsdale House School and is the oldest girls' school in the city.

UNTHANK ROAD, p.u. 1914

Looking back along Unthank Road towards the city. On the left is the sign of Fred Perowne, watchmaker & jeweller; next is H.R. Barley, shoemaker; and in the centre the 'Park Tavern' public house, now the 'Lilley Langtry'. The tram is on the Unthank Road/Magdalen Road route and has stopped by the junction with Park Lane to allow passengers to alight. On the right, in the foreground, is the junction with Trinity Street.

UNTHANK ROAD, p.u. 1915

Photographed very near to the previous location on page 19, but looking in the opposite direction towards Colman Road. Gloucester Street Post Office is on the left and the junction with Dover Street can be seen centre right.

Notice the two workmen repairing the road, the steam-roller and horse-drawn vehicles in the distance; and in the foreground, the tram stop sign 'Cars stop here when required', and the Gloucester Street sign at the top of the lamp post.

THE JENNY LIND HOSPITAL, c. 1911

The Jenny Lind Hospital was situated on the corner of Unthank Road and Colman Road. It was opened in 1900 by the Prince and Princess of Wales (later King Edward VII and Queen Alexandra). It served as the Children's Hospital for Norwich and later, the building was substantially altered to become the Colman Hospital.

THE JENNY LIND HOSPITAL, c. 1908

Published by T. Hopper of Leopold Road, Norwich, and showing one of the children's wards.
The postcard was sent by one of the nurses and the message on the reverse reads, "This is part of one of the Surgical Wards
(23 beds) taken at Christmas time. The matron is standing next to me and one of the sisters is further on".

NEWMARKET ROAD, c. 1910

Newmarket Road, part of the A11 trunk road, is one of the most impressive roads leading into Norwich.
Photographed close to the junction with Daniels Road and viewed looking towards the city.
Many trees in this area suffered hurricane damage in October, 1987.

Eaton Road, Norwich.

EATON ROAD, c. 1915

Eaton Road lies between Newmarket Road and Ipswich Road and runs nearly parallel with, and to the south of, Daniels Road.

The City of Norwich School completed in 1910 (now the Eaton C.N.S. School) is just out of view on the left.

THE FOUNTAIN, c. 1910

The Fountain was situated at the junction of Ipswich and Newmarket Roads. The brick tower with its four arches, four pediments and pyramid-shaped roof protected the figure of a young woman and child, designed by J.E. Boehm in 1874. The statue was moved to the grounds of the Norfolk and Norwich Hospital to make way for road improvements, and the brick tower was demolished in the 1950s.
The junction with Grove Road can be seen on the extreme left.

GROVE ROAD, c. 1907
An almost deserted view of Grove Road looking towards St. Stephen's Road.
The row of houses on the right remain, but the left-hand row of houses have been demolished and replaced with modern town houses.

Llandaff House.

LLANDAFF HOUSE, GROVE ROAD, c. 1910

Llandaff House was a private girls' school for boarders and day pupils and was situated on the corner of Victoria Street and Grove Road.

In 1926, Llandaff House became the City of Norwich Children's Home. The building was bombed during the Second World War and the site is now part of a modern housing development.

THE NORFOLK AND NORWICH HOSPITAL, c. 1910

The Norfolk and Norwich Hospital facing St. Stephen's Road was built between 1770 and 1775 and designed by William Ivory. A new wing was added in 1802.

On 17th June, 1879, H.R.H. The Prince of Wales (later King Edward VII) laid the foundation stone for the new administration block, shown in the centre of the postcard.

The iron railings in front of the Hospital still remain.

THE NORFOLK & NORWICH HOSPITAL, NORWICH

THE NORFOLK AND NORWICH HOSPITAL, c. 1930

An aerial photograph showing the H-shaped design of the Hospital and the surrounding roads.
The administration block and the Leicester Nurses' Home can be seen centre and centre left respectively.
At the top of the photograph, in the centre, the roads are Nicholas Street and Shadwell Street. These two roads have now disappeared due to hospital re-development.
Crookes Place is visible on the right.

THE LEICESTER NURSES' HOME

The Leicester Nurses' Home was situated within the grounds of the Norfolk and Norwich Hospital. It was built in 1903 for the use of nursing staff and private nurses.
The building still stands today but has altered slightly due to bomb damage in 1942-43.

LEICESTER STREET, c. 1912

Leicester Street connects York Street to Onley Street and lies between Unthank Road and Newmarket Road, close to the Norfolk and Norwich Hospital.
This photograph is typical of the times, showing a deserted street scene.

NEWMARKET STREET, c. 1912

Newmarket Street runs parallel with Leicester Street and this view has been photographed from Brunswick Road looking south-west towards Mount Pleasant. It remains much the same today, apart from the motor cars now parked along the street.

Victoria
Garage,
St. Stephen's
Road,
Norwich.
(On main
London Road.)

*Granville Duff,
Manager.*

Telegraphic address,
"Garage", Norwich.

Telephone No. 451,
Norwich.

ST. STEPHEN'S ROAD, c. 1910
An advertising postcard showing the workshop belonging to the Victoria Garage, situated on St. Stephen's Road, close to Victoria Station. This old garage stood on part of the site now occupied by Sedgwick's offices.
Postcards similar to the one shown would have been used to advise customers of the various services offered by the garage.
Can anyone identify the splendid selection of motor cars?

8733   GREAT EASTERN RAILWAY. VICTORIA STATION. NORWICH.

VICTORIA STATION, c. 1912

Victoria Station was built by the Eastern Union Railway on the site of the old Victoria Gardens, between St. Stephen's Road, Queen's Road and Grove Road.

On 7th November, 1849, the first passenger train, named 'Goliath', departed at 11.13 a.m. on its journey to Ipswich. The train pulled a goods wagon with a band and fifteen carriages with 550 people inside.

Victoria Station was closed to passenger traffic in May 1916, with passenger services taken over by Thorpe Station. It operated as a goods depot and following bomb damage during the Second World War, the depot closed completely. The old goods depot site is now occupied by Sedgwick's Offices and the coal yard on the other side of Grove Road is to be a Sainsbury superstore.

CHAPEL FIELD GARDENS,
NORWICH.

CHAPEL FIELD GARDENS, c. 1912

In 1880, an archery and drill ground of 8½ acres was converted by the City Corporation into public pleasure gardens, known as Chapel Field Gardens.

One of the unusual structures, which stood in the middle of the Gardens, was the Pagoda. This elaborate cast-iron pavilion was designed by Thomas Jeckyll and manufactured by Barnard, Bishop and Barnard of Norwich for the Philadelphia exhibition of 1876. The Pagoda was later demolished in 1949.

On the right is the old bandstand, which is rarely used today.

F.G. STONE, LAME DOG, QUEEN'S ROAD NORWICH,
4 SEATER TOURING CAR FOR HIRE. TELEPHONE No. 1148.

QUEEN'S ROAD, c. 1920

A rare and collectable postcard showing a magnificent four-seater open-topped touring car owned and offered for hire by Mr. F.G. Stone.

The photograph was taken outside the 'Lame Dog' public house at 68, Queen's Road. The 'Lame Dog' was a typical corner public house owned by Morgan's Brewery and situated by the junction of Queen's Road and All Saint's Green, then called Upper Surrey Street.

Later, the 'Lame Dog' closed and the site was cleared to make way for the widening of Queen's Road as part of the inner link road.

BRACONDALE, c. 1912

The Richmond Hill Tavern, owned by Bullard's Brewery, was situated at 1, Bracondale, an early Georgian town house. The 'bottle and jug' entrance is on the right and the window poster advertises a Norwich City v Millwall match at the Nest. The building remains today but is now a private house.

ST. STEPHEN'S STREET, c. 1906

Looking towards the city centre and showing the upper part of St. Stephen's Street, which has changed beyond all recognition since the street was widened after the Second World War.

In the left foreground is 'The Trumpet' public house, on the corner of Coburg Street, and on the right is The Bull Inn, close to the junction with Bull Lane.

The Rose Tavern is behind the tram, number 24, which is on the Thorpe Road to Newmarket Road route.

THE BOAR'S HEAD, NORWICH

THE BOAR'S HEAD INN, c. 1904

The old thatched Boar's Head Inn was situated on the corner of Surrey Street and St. Stephen's Street. The building dated back to the mid-15th century and was the home of Richard Brown, a city Alderman. In the 17th and 18th centuries, it became the 'Greyhound' and was renamed the Boar's Head Inn in the early 19th century, after it was purchased by Mr. John Norgate. Notice the sign on the corner, 'Norgate & Son, Agents for Bass, Ind Coope & Co., and Guinness'. Until c. 1870, the front of the building facing St. Stephen's Street was a grocer's shop.
In the early 20th century, the Boar's Head Inn was sold to Diver & Son, who restored the building. It burnt down in April, 1942 during the Norwich Blitz.

St. Stephen's Street, Norwich

ST. STEPHEN'S STREET, c. 1920

A busy scene at the lower end of St. Stephen's Street and photographed by the junctions with Westlegate and Rampant Horse Street.

In the centre, to the right of the tram, is Row and Taylor, chemists, and on the right, Buntings store, previously the site of Arthur Henning & Co., which is now occupied by Marks and Spencers.

DEACONS RESTAURANT, c. 1930

Deacons Restaurant was situated on the corner of Westlegate and Red Lion Street. The business was established in 1910 and this publicity postcard advertises Deacons new Restaurant as 'the most up-to-date Restaurant in Norwich'.

Since Deacons closed, the building has been occupied by various furniture and carpet shops and is now occupied by Harvey's Linen Shop.

MOST UP-TO-DATE RESTAURANT IN NORWICH

FISH   JOINTS   GRILLS

DAINTY AFTERNOON TEAS   CATERING

FISH, GAME AND POULTRY MERCHANTS

ST. STEPHEN'S PLAIN & WESTLEGATE

TEL. NORWICH 230

WESTLEGATE, c. 1912

All Saints' Church lies at the top of Westlegate, close to All Saint's Green, and was built in the 15th century.

At the time the photograph was taken, the buildings on the left were occupied by: No. 14, Carter Paterson; No. 16, a private house; No. 18, Richard Ranson, bootmaker; and No. 20, Arthur Kemp, greengrocer, who occupied the thatched gabled building with the hand cart outside.

In the 19th century, number 20, Westlegate was the 'Light Dragoon' public house, commonly known as the 'Barking Dicky'. In more recent years, it was occupied by Williams and Glyn's Bank, and is now the offices for the Prime Financial Business Bureau.

Since the late 1960's, All Saints' Church has been in the care of the Norfolk branch of the Mother's Union, and the 15th-century font has been moved to St. Julian's Church.

ALL SAINTS' GREEN, c. 1915

Viewed towards Westlegate and showing the buildings which lined the eastern side of All Saints' Green. Many of these buildings date from the eighteenth and early nineteenth centuries, but the lower thatched building with its projecting bay windows is of particular interest.

The building known as the Thatched Assembly Rooms was restored extensively by Major Crow at the turn of this century, to become an outstanding suite of ball and assembly rooms.

On 11th November, 1915, it became the Thatched Cinema, which later closed in 1930. It was purchased by R.H. Bond & Sons, who converted the building to adjoin their existing store, and re-opened as a restaurant, ballroom and furnishing hall. On 27th June, 1942, Bond's store and the Assembly Rooms were destroyed by incendiary bombs.

THE LAMB INN, ORFORD PLACE, c. 1905

The Lamb Inn is one of the oldest Norwich hostelries. It was the scene of the brutal murder of the landlord, John Aggas, by his brother-in-law, Timothy Hardy, in November, 1787.
This early postcard shows one of the horse-drawn carriers which operated from the Lamb Inn's yard, off Orford Place.

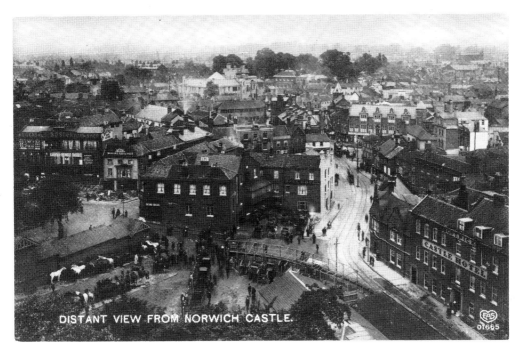

A DISTANT VIEW FROM NORWICH CASTLE, c. 1910

Looking in a southerly direction and showing Castle Hill, Red Lion Street with its double row of tram-lines, and part of Castle Meadow on the right.

In the foreground, on the left, is the old Horse Market. In the centre is the Bell Hotel, before it was painted white and owned for a time by Trust House hotels. To the left of the Bell Hotel is the Napier Tavern, a Morgan's public house, and Boston's furniture store.

V290-3   NORWICH. THE CASTLE.   RAPID PHOTO. E.C.

NORWICH CASTLE AND CATTLE MARKET, c. 1920s

Norwich Castle is believed to have been founded by Ralph de Guader, who was made Earl of East Anglia by William the Conqueror. The early castle was made of wood and the stone keep was not built until c. 1160. Gradually, over the years, the castle became less important as a fortress and was used as a gaol until c. 1887. The keep was completely refaced in Bath stone in 1833-9.

In 1887, the Norwich Corporation purchased the Castle and converted the keep into a Museum, which opened in 1894. The Castle Museum is exceptional and contains many fine exhibits of local interest, a splendid collection of birds, and the Castle Art Galleries, which includes the famous Colman Collection added in 1951.

The Cattle Market, held on the levelled former outer defences of the Castle for over 300 years, was moved to its new site in Hall Road and opened on 1st July, 1960. The site is now a car park.

THE ROYAL ARCADE, c. 1910

An unusual view of the Royal Arcade, designed in an Art Nouveau style by the Norwich architect, George Skipper, and built in 1900.

The Royal Arcade joins Castle Street with Gentleman's Walk. The front of the Arcade facing the Market Place is plain, but the real architectural gem is the facade facing Castle Street.

In the left foreground can be seen part of the 'Arcade' public house.

THE ARCADE, NORWICH

47

S 8731   SHIRE HALL, NORWICH.

THE SHIRE HALL, c. 1910

The Shire Hall was designed by William Wilkins and built in a Tudor style between 1822 and 1823, along Castle Meadow and Market Avenue. The Shire Hall was enlarged in 1887 and 1908, and refaced in 1913.
The Assizes and Quarter Sessions were held at the Shire Hall, and later, the Crown Court was held here until June, 1988.
The cattle pens, seen in the foreground, have now been converted into a grassed area.

All Risks taken.

Please send for Price List.

THE SHIREHALL, NORWICH.

THE SHIRE HALL, c. 1912

An advertising postcard for the Norwich Window & Carpet Cleaning Co., owned by W.H. Sellex. Their services also included carpet-beating, coal and coke supplies and removals.

THE BOER WAR MEMORIAL, 1904

The Boer War Memorial stands facing Prince of Wales Road and adjacent to the Shire Hall, and was built at a cost of £1,600. The War Memorial, dedicated to the 300 men of Norfolk who lost their lives in the Boer War, was unveiled by Major-General Wynne on 17th November, 1904. The ceremony was attended by civic dignitaries and vast crowds.

TOMBLAND FAIR, c. 1907

A fair has been held in the city since the 12th century. The mediaeval fair was held at Whitsun on Tombland, and has been known ever since as Tombland Fair.

Later, Tombland Fair was held at Easter and by the middle of the last century, it was held on the old Cattle Market. The fair is still held annually and in 1988 it was moved out to the new Cattle Market site on Hall Road.

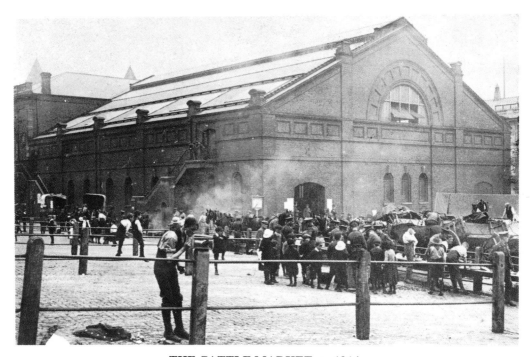

THE CATTLE MARKET, c. 1914

Photographed from the Cattle Market and showing the back of the Agricultural Hall and soldiers of the Essex Regiment.
In the foreground, notice the soldier shaving, and on the right, the group of soldiers washing, with many children looking on.
The Agricultural Hall was designed by J. Pearce and built in 1882. It is now occupied by Anglia Television.

FAT STOCK SHOW, 1934
One of the prize cattle from the Fat Stock Show held at the Agricultural Hall in 1934. This area is now grassed over.

CATTLE MARKET STREET, c. 1906

Cattle Market Street leads from Rose Lane to Golden Ball Street, and is now part of the city's one-way system.
On the left is E.A. Bennett, wholesale corn, hay and straw merchant. Further along is 'The Lion' public house owned by
Youngs, Crawshay and Youngs, and in the background, on the right, is part of the Cattle Market.

THE OLD MUSIC HOUSE, c. 1908

The Old Music House was built originally as a private house for a wealthy Jewish family in the 12th century and is reputed to be the oldest house in Norwich. In 1487, the property was purchased by Sir John Paston, to whom the grand hall is attributed. In 1584, the house was acquired by Sir Edward Coke, later Lord Chief Justice, through his marriage to Bridget Paston.

Later, the house became an inn, called the Old Music House, and at the time of this photograph, it was owned by Youngs, Crawshay and Youngs Brewery.

It is now known as Wensum Lodge owned by the Norfolk County Council and used as a residential education centre.

V290-18   NORWICH. BANK PLAIN AND LONDON STREET.   RAPID PHOTO. E C

BANK PLAIN, c. 1912

Photographed at the junction with London Street. On the right, one of the shops was occupied by Hayward Kidd, printers,
stationers and tobacconists, who published many local postcards including those for Norwich City Football Club.
Further to the left of the picture and out of view, the impressive building owned by Barclays Bank was designed by
E. Boardman and Brierly and Rutherford and built in 1929–31.

G.P.O. AND PRINCE OF
WALES ROAD, NORWICH

PRINCE OF WALES ROAD, c. 1912

Prince of Wales Road was constructed in the mid-19th century and many fine Victorian houses were built along its route. When Thorpe Station was built in 1886, it served to link the station with the city centre.
On the left of the picture is the Royal Hotel, built in 1896-97. The nearest building on the right is the front of the Agricultural Hall, and to its left is the old Post Office which was originally built as the Crown Bank in 1866. Both buildings have been joined together and are now occupied by the headquarters of Anglia Television.

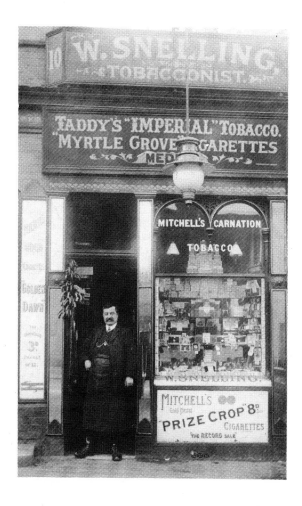

10, PRINCE OF WALES ROAD

A very rare postcard of W. Snelling, tobacconist, who occupied 10, Prince of Wales Road.

The shop front displays some splendid advertisements which include: Taddy's 'Imperial' Tobacco; 'Myrtle Grove' cigarettes; Mitchell's 'Golden Dawn' cigarettes (3d for 12); and Mitchell's 'Prize Crop' cigarettes (8d per packet). Notice the lamp above the shop.

This old shop is now part of the 'Prince of Wales' public house.

The author has a personal interest in this card because his mother worked here for several years after the First World War, and spoke of seeing Nurse Edith Cavell's funeral procession pass here on its way to Norwich Cathedral.

92, PRINCE OF WALES ROAD, c. 1912

A detailed photograph of the Travel Bureau, 92, Prince of Wales Road. The postcard shows an arrangement of advertising posters for all the major shipping companies. Notice the travel time between London and Paris of 6 hours, 50 minutes.

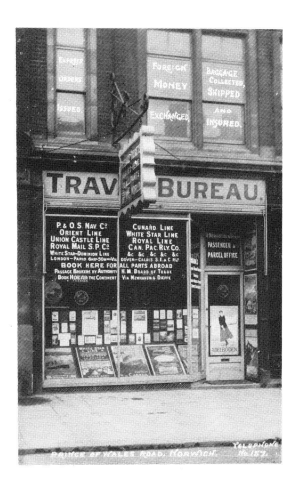

PRINCE OF WALES ROAD, c. 1906

Looking up Prince of Wales Road towards the city centre, and photographed from Foundry Bridge which was built in 1844.
On the extreme right is the corner of the 'Norfolk Railway House', a Bullard's public house.
Notice the horse-drawn parcels delivery van in the centre of the picture.

RIVERSIDE, c. 1912

A view of the River Wensum and Riverside looking towards Foundry Bridge and Thorpe Road.
Ransons Ltd., timber merchants, shown on the left, had their main entrance on Mountergate. Timber would have been
carried by barge to and from their warehouse facing the river.

BILLY BLUELIGHT.

BILLY BLUELIGHT

Billy Bluelight, whose real name was William Cullum, was born in 1859 and was one of Norwich's great characters.

One of his favourite jaunts was to race the 'Jenny Lind' on its journey from Foundry Bridge to Yarmouth; a distance of some twenty miles. When the 'Jenny Lind' arrived in Yarmouth, he would be waiting by the quayside to meet the passengers who would make a collection for him.

He was eccentric in dress, often wearing a top hat and white plimsolls, and would be seen on Gentleman's Walk selling wild flowers and cough sweets.

Billy Bluelight died in 1949 aged 90 years.

S.S. 'JENNY LIND', c. 1912
The S.S. 'Jenny Lind' on one of its pleasure trips on the River Yare between Norwich and Yarmouth.

PULL'S FERRY, c. 1906

An unusual view of Pull's Ferry, one of the city's best known landmarks, which stands on the west bank of the River Wensum at the end of the Cathedral Close.

It dates back to the fifteenth century and served as a water-gate over a canal, built from the river to the Cathedral Close and used to transport the Caen stone for the building of the Cathedral. The canal was filled in during the 18th century.

Pull's Ferry was also known as Sandlin's Ferry, after a chorister in the reign of Elizabeth I. The house adjoining the water-gate dates from the 17th century, and later became an inn in the 19th century.

Pull's Ferry was named after John Pull, who was appointed keeper of the Ferry in 1796, and also the last landlord of the inn. The Ferry closed in the 1930s and the house was restored by money raised by the Norwich Girl Guides in c. 1950.

BISHOP'S BRIDGE AND THE RIVER WENSUM, c. 1906

Bishop's Bridge, spanning the River Wensum, is Norwich's oldest bridge and was built in c. 1340 by Richard Spynk who also built most of the City Walls and other defences. Originally, the bridge belonged to the Prior of the Cathedral, but in 1393 the ownership was transferred to the citizens of Norwich.

The bridge, constructed mainly in flint, has three low arches of stone and brick. A massive gateway with turrets stood at the western end, until it was demolished in 1790. The bridge was also the scene of fierce fighting during Kett's Rebellion in 1549.

This view is taken looking north towards Bishop's Bridge and shows the 'Red Lion' public house in the background.

MARION ROAD, c. 1912

Looking up Marion Road from its junction with Hill House Road, off Rosary Road.
The view remains much the same today, with the exception of the new Marion Road Day Centre which is situated on the
left, at the top of Marion Road.

THE COW TOWER, c. 1910

The Cow Tower was built in c. 1378 as part of the city's defences. The tower, 50ft high and 36 ft wide at its base, guarded the north-east corner of the city by protecting the sharp bend of the River Wensum.
The Cow Tower was used as a tollhouse and controlled the river traffic entering the city. The tower has also been used as a prison.

MOUSEHOLD HEATH, c. 1912

Mousehold Heath offers spectacular views of the city. It was the scene of the encampment of twenty thousand rebels at the time of Robert Kett's rebellion in 1549.

This photograph shows a tram descending Gurney Road with St. James Hill and Spitalfields on the right.

In the background, on the right, is part of the Britannia Barracks built in 1885-87. The site is now occupied by Norwich Prison and the home of the Royal Norfolk Regimental Museum.

THE CAVALRY BARRACKS, c. 1913

The Cavalry Barracks, or Nelson Barracks, were built in 1791 on the site of an old manor house. They were situated in Barrack Street, and at one time they were occupied by five hundred men of all ranks with stabling for three hundred and forty horses.

The Barracks were demolished in 1966 to make way for a housing development.

MAGDALEN ROAD, c. 1912

Looking north along Magdalen Road and photographed at the junctions with Magpie Road and Bull Close Road.
The entrances to Stacey Road and Marlborough Road can be seen on the left and right respectively.
The old Divisional Police Station stands on the right and part of the 'Artichoke' public house can just be seen.

GUERNSEY ROAD, c. 1910

Guernsey Road lies between Heath Road and Magdalen Road. The photograph shows typical rows of terraced houses and a few local children who have posed for the camera.
The postcard was probably produced to sell in a local shop.

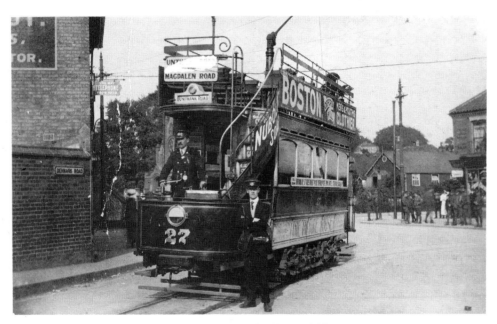

DENMARK ROAD, c. 1914

A superb study of a tram, complete with its driver and conductor, parked by the entrance to Denmark Road, close to the junctions with Sprowston Road and Silver Road, before its departure to Unthank Road.
The upper advertisement on the side of the tram reads, 'Boston, Timber Hill, Men and Youth's Clothier'; and the lower advertisement gives details about the Haymarket Picture House.
Notice the 'You may telephone from here' sign top left, and the group of soldiers standing by the corner shop on the right.
Trams first operated in Norwich in 1901.

MAGDALEN STREET, c. 1908

Magdalen Street is one of the oldest streets in Norwich. This view, looking towards the city, shows Magdalen Street close to the junction with Bull Close Road, seen in the left foreground.

The shops on the left-hand side of the street include: Nicholls Bros., bakers; an ironmonger; and W. Gibson, hairdresser. On the right hand side, the shops include: William Pimm, grocers; Hugh McQuire, newsagent; J. Reeves, leather stores; and Frank Schofield, butcher.

In 1958, Magdalen Street was selected by the Civic Trust for an extensive scheme of redecoration and repair.

MAGDALEN STREET, NORWICH. — BOXING MORNING, 1906.

MAGDALEN STREET, 1906

One of the few snow scenes of Norwich produced as a postcard. Five trams can be seen parked outside the Phoenix Shoe Works, which occupied 96-100 Magdalen Street. This building was a Georgian mansion occupied at one time by John Patteson, Mayor of Norwich in 1823.

The Phoenix Shoe Works later became Hurrell's shoe factory which was damaged by fire during an air raid in August 1942. The factory was rebuilt after the Second World War on the same site, but was demolished at the end of the 1960s to make way for the new shops in Anglia Square.

COLEGATE, c. 1909

Looking westwards towards Duke Street. The 'Black Boys' public house on the left has now been renamed the 'Merchants Tavern'. Further down, also on the left, is the Norvic Shoe Factory (Howlett and Whites) – now converted into offices. In the centre is Bacon's House built in the mid-16th century by Henry Bacon, Mayor of Norwich (1557, 1566). Behind Bacon's House is the tower of St. George's Church. Perpendicular in design, the tower and nave were built c. 1459, the chancel c. 1498, and the aisles and chapel c. 1510. The interior of the church contains 18th century furnishings, an interesting font and a memorial to John Crome, the founder of the Norwich School of Painting.

Many merchants built their houses in Colegate between the 17th and 19th centuries.

Quaint Old Norwich, Rosemary Lane

ROSEMARY LANE, c. 1910

This postcard is one of a series entitled 'Quaint Old Norwich'.

The view of Rosemary Lane is taken looking towards St. Michael's Alley and Colegate. The steps to St. Michael's Alley are in the background, behind the children. Some of the buildings shown have now been restored.

ELM HILL, c. 1910

Today Elm Hill is one of the picturesque areas in Norwich, with its quaint buildings, alleys and cobbled streets.

At the time of this photograph, the area was very run down and many parts were to be demolished. Through the excellent work of the Norwich Society, Elm Hill was extensively restored after 1926.

This view looks towards Wagon and Horses Lane, with the Cathedral spire just seen above the rooftops.

The small elm tree was replaced by a London plane tree in 1986 after the elm tree became infected with Dutch elm disease.

Quaint Old Norwich, Elm Hill

NORWICH. ANGUISH'S HOUSE. NOW MAID'S HEAD HOTEL

V290·1   RAPID PHOTO. E C

THE MAID'S HEAD HOTEL, p.u. 1909

The Maid's Head Hotel stands on the corner of Tombland and Wensum Street. It is the oldest hostelry in East Anglia, and probably the sixth oldest hostelry in England. The building dates from c. 1287 when it was kept by monks as a hospice attached to the Bishop's Palace. During Edward III's reign it was known as the Myrtle Fish Tavern, and in 1578, it is alleged that Queen Elizabeth 1 slept here.

The building was restored during the 18th century and altered again in the 19th century by building a mock Tudor front which exists today.

Inside the Maid's Head Hotel, the original bar is used as a parlour with access through a roofed courtyard.

TOMBLAND, NORWICH

TOMBLAND, c. 1906

The name Tombland derives from the word 'tomb', or open land. Originally, Tombland was the old market place, but today, it serves as a spacious square lined with many Georgian houses.

This early view shows the eastern side of Tombland with Upper Close and the Cathedral behind the houses. On the left is the Erpingham Gate, one of the entrances into Upper Close, built in 1420 in memory of St. Thomas Erpingham who commanded the English archers at the battle of Agincourt in 1415.

The tram is on the Magdalen Road to Earlham Road route. Notice the horse-drawn landau on the right.

1036 Nurse Cavell Memorial, Norwich

NURSE CAVELL'S MEMORIAL

This statue is a memorial to Nurse Edith Cavell, erected in Tombland and paid for by public subscription. It was unveiled by H.M. Queen Alexandra on 12th October, 1918.

Edith Cavell was one of Norfolk's famous heroines, born at Swardeston in 1865, the daughter of the Rector. She started her nursing career in 1896 and in August 1914 went to Brussels to organise the nursing of wounded soldiers. She helped many stranded soldiers to escape to neutral Holland, and was arrested by the enemy in August 1915, tried and found guilty. Edith Cavell was shot by the Germans on 12th October, 1915.

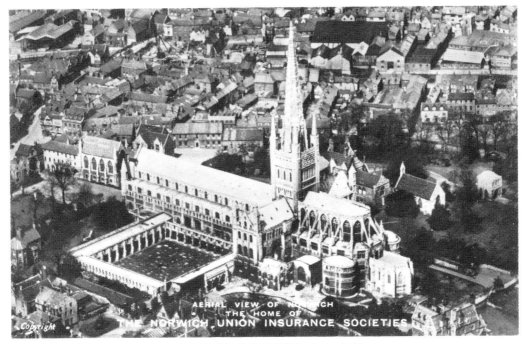

NORWICH CATHEDRAL, c. 1930

The Cathedral Church of the Holy and Undivided Trinity was founded by the first Bishop of Norwich, Herbert de Losinga in 1096. The early church, a superb example of Norman architecture and constructed with Barnack and Caen stone, was completed during the early 12th century, and later consecrated in 1278.

Between the 13th and 16th centuries, the Norman church had numerous additions to become the magnificent Cathedral, which is the pride of East Anglia.

The Cathedral is cruciform in shape and 407 ft long. Above the nave is a splendid vaulted roof, which replaced a wooden roof destroyed by fire, with its remarkable series of 328 sculptured bosses illustrating scenes from the Creation to the Judgement. The 15th-century spire, the second highest in England, is 315 ft high and replaced an earlier wooden spire destroyed by a hurricane in 1362.

The cloisters, the largest in England, were rebuilt between 1297 and 1420.

During this century, the War Memorial Chapel was completed in 1932, and the organ was rebuilt after its destruction by fire before the Second World War.

ST. AUGUSTINE'S STREET, c. 1905

A view of St. Augustine's Street looking towards Aylsham Road and the junction with Bakers Road.
The premises from left to right are: No. 64 – 'Royal Oak' public house; No. 66 – Mrs A. Elsegood, butcher; St. Martin at
Oak Wall Lane; No. 68 – J.C. Cook, boot and shoemaker, and St. Augustine's sub-post office; No. 70 – Girling, fruiterer;
and No. 72 – The 'Staff of Life' public house.

ST. AUGUSTINE'S GATE AND SCHOOL, c. 1930

St. Augustine's School was situated by St. Augustine's Gate on the corner of Green Hills and Infirmary Road, now known as Aylsham Road and Waterloo Road respectively. The school was destroyed during the air raids of 1942, and the site is now occupied by the Norwich Swimming Baths which were built in 1959-61.
In the centre can be seen H. Bishop's shoe shop, which still occupies the same premises today.

THE MAGPIE PUBLIC HOUSE, c. 1915

The 'Magpie' public house was situated next to Catherine Wheel Opening, near Magpie Road.
The notice, to the left of the door, reads, 'Public Weighbridge authorised by Norwich Council'. The weighbridge can be seen in the foreground.
The building remains much the same today, although the weighbridge has now been removed.

AYLSHAM ROAD, p.u. 1914

Looking in a north-westerly direction away from the city centre and showing the entrance to Berners Street on the left and Vicarage Road on the right. Upper Hellesdon Post Office is on the corner of Berners Street.

Midland and Great Northern (City) Station, Norwich.

CITY STATION, c. 1912

City Station served as the terminus for the Midland and Great Northern Railway. The station was opened in December 1882 and was situated close to the River Wensum, facing Station Road which linked Barn Road and Oak Street.

The twin towers, either side of the station, were occupied by offices on one side and the Station Master's house on the other. The central archway led to a roadway, 200 ft long, with two platforms, 700 ft long, either side.

The station was severely damaged during the 1942 blitz. It re-opened after the War and served as a goods depot, finally closing in the late 1950s. The site is now occupied in part by the roundabout on the inner link road which joins Barn Road with St. Crispins Road.

DEREHAM ROAD, c. 1906

An amazing view which has changed beyond all recognition. The clue to its exact location is the 'Gatehouse' public house, which is on the right, just before the junction with Hellesdon Road.
The area is now completely built up.

DEREHAM ROAD, p.u. 1910

Looking towards the city centre and photographed near the junction with Old Palace Road. On the left is the shop belonging to C.W. Clarke, corn merchant, and further down is the entrance to Exeter Road. On the right is the 'Lord John Russell' public house.

ST. BENEDICT'S STREET, c. 1910

The western end of St. Benedict's Street photographed in front of the remains of the old gatehouse to St. Benedict's Gate, which abutted the end of St. Benedict's Street and later demolished after the air raids of April, 1942. (St. Benedict's Gate was demolished in 1793).

This view looks towards the city centre and shows in the left foreground: No. 85 – Baldwin, newsagent; No. 83 – Walker's; No. 81 – Farrow, butcher; and No. 79 – Hicks, fishmonger. Further down, on the left of the tram, was the 'Beehive' public house.

On the right, the premises in the foreground are Nos. 100–108. No. 108 was occupied by a barber's shop (notice the striped pole), later demolished in 1938.

F. W. Harmer & Co., St. Andrews Works, Norwich

ST. ANDREW STREET

F.W. Harmer & Co., clothing manufacturers, were founded in 1825 and occupied St. Andrew's Works in St. Andrew Street. During both World Wars, the factory manufactured uniforms. The building was destroyed by fire during an air raid on 18th March, 1943.

Harmer & Co. are still clothing manufacturers today with their factory in Havers Road.

St. Andrew Street was widened in 1966 and the site of the old clothing factory is now occupied by part of the new Telephone Exchange and an open space.

STRANGERS' HALL, c. 1912

Strangers' Hall was built in the 16th century on the site of an earlier hall, built by Ralph de Middleton in the 14th century. The 16th-century hall was the home of Nicholas Sotherton, a grocer, who later became Mayor in 1539. The Hall contains some splendid features which include the 14th-century vaulted undercroft, the remains of the earlier hall; the 15th-century Banqueting Hall built by William Barley, a local merchant; the Carolean staircase c. 1627; and the beautiful oriel window.

There is a legend that Strangers' Hall was named after sheltering Flemish weavers during the reign of Queen Elizabeth I, having fled from Spanish persecution in the Netherlands. Strangers' Hall became the Judges' Lodgings in the 18th century, a Roman Catholic presbytery in the 19th century, and in 1922, the hall was presented to the city by Mr. Leonard G. Bollingbroke. Strangers' Hall is now a museum of English domestic life through the ages.

The front of the building faces Charing Cross and the rear overlooks St. Gregory's Alley.

Free Library, Norwich.

THE FREE LIBRARY, c. 1910

The Free Library opened in 1857 and stood on the corner of St. Andrew and Duke Streets.

The Library closed in 1963 and moved to the new Central Public Library in Bethel Street, opened the same year by H.M. Queen Elizabeth the Queen Mother.

VISIT OF H.M. KING EDWARD VII TO NORWICH, 1909

His Majesty King Edward VII is seen leaving the Drill Hall on the corner of Chapelfield and Chapelfield North, after presenting colours to various units of the Territorial Army on 25th October, 1909.

After lunch at the Drill Hall, the King went to the Norfolk & Norwich Hospital to lay the foundation stone for the new observation and septic block.

During this visit to Norfolk, the King stayed at Quidenham Hall as the guest of Lord and Lady Albemarle.

VISIT OF H.M. KING GEORGE V TO NORWICH, 1911

On 28th June, 1911, six days after his Coronation, H.M. King George V visited Norwich for the Royal Agricultural Show at Crown Point, Trowse.

The postcard shows the King on the way to St. Andrew's Hall via Bank Plain to meet distinguished guests, and to receive his official welcome from the Lord Mayor of Norwich.

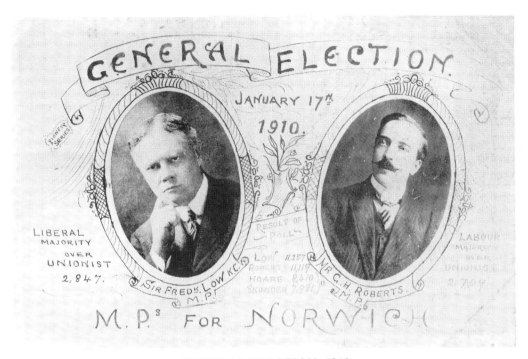

GENERAL ELECTION, 1910

Postcards were used as an effective way of conveying local news. This card gives the result of the General Election held on 17th January, 1910. The two successful Members of Parliament for Norwich were Sir Frederick Low, K.C., M.P. (Liberal) and Mr. G.H. Roberts, M.P. (Labour).

CARROW WORKS, c. 1910

Jeremiah Colman founded his business in 1805, after taking over an old mill at Stoke Holy Cross to manufacture mustard.
His great nephew, Jeremiah James Colman, transferred the business to Carrow Works in 1856, after building new mills which gave better access to rail and river transportation.
At the time of this postcard, Colman's employed about 3,000 staff in mustard, starch and cornflour production.
In the centre can be seen the old Carrow Bridge, which was demolished when the new Carrow Bridge was built in 1922.
The new bridge was officially opened by H.R.H. The Prince of Wales in 1923.

LAKENHAM MILL FIRE, 1908

Lakenham Mill was situated at the foot of Long John Hill and was owned by Mr. Hollige.
A fire started in the mill at about midnight on 31st March, 1908. A messenger was sent by pony to alert the City Fire Brigade, but by the time he had arrived in the city, and the Fire Brigade had mobilised and returned to the mill, the building had been completely destroyed. It was reported that the flames could be seen from Norwich Market Place.

BRETT'S FACTORY FIRE, 1909

The factory belonging to John Brett & Son, Ltd., furniture manufacturers, was situated between Paddock Street, Barker Street and Heigham Street.

During the morning of Sunday, 15th August, 1909, a fire started in the factory which quickly engulfed the whole building. Large crowds gathered to watch the blaze. Firemen were able to rescue a few items of furniture, which were either placed in the streets or nearby houses not threatened by the fire. The factory was completely destroyed and although the fire was under control by 3 p.m., firemen were on the scene for many hours afterwards clearing the debris.

THE COCK INN, LAKENHAM, c. 1906

The old thatched Cock Inn photographed close to the bridge crossing the River Yare. At the time, the Cock Inn served ales and stouts brewed by Steward and Patteson's brewery.

THE COCK INN, LAKENHAM, 1908

On 31st March, 1908, a major fire occured which almost destroyed the Cock Inn. The fire was caused by sparks, blown by a strong wind from the mill nearby, igniting the thatched roof of the Cock Inn and the adjacent house. The resultant blaze could be seen for miles around. A few items of furniture were saved including a painting of the landlord, Mr. Bird.

THE COCK INN, LAKENHAM, c. 1911

The rebuilt Cock Inn photographed about three years after the fire. On the left, by the bridge, Lakenham Post Office was part of an old cottage built in the early 18th century.

Norwich Floods, August 27/12. Orchard Street. J. & S. 7794.

THE NORWICH FLOODS, 1912

On 27th August, 1912, seven inches of rainfall caused severe flooding in the city. The Norwich Floods disaster resulted in extensive damage and two deaths: a baby, who fell from a mother's arms during their rescue, and George Brodie, who lost his footing and drowned after saving several people.

This postcard, one of a series, shows Orchard Street with one of Price's horse-drawn bread vans making deliveries to residents after the floods.

THE NORWICH FLOODS, 1912

The Norwich Floods were photographed extensively and published on many postcards by various local publishers; at least 200 different postcards are known to exist.

This view shows Magdalen Street and its junction with Colegate on the left. Horses and carts were the only reliable transport around the streets. Notice the people looking down on the activity below from their first-floor windows.

Upper Hellesdon Mill, Norwich.

UPPER HELLESDON MILL, c. 1906

Upper Hellesdon Mill stood in Press Lane, off Aylsham Road. It was built in the 1870s replacing an earlier post mill, and was owned by Mr. Ephtain Witard, one of the best known millers in Norwich.

The photograph for this rare postcard was taken shortly before the mill burnt down.

THE MILL, CRINGLEFORD, N^R NORWICH.

CRINGLEFORD MILL, c. 1912

This large corn mill stood by the River Yare. The original mill was built during the 12th century. It was destroyed by fire during the early 16th century, rebuilt in 1541, but destroyed again by fire in 1916. All that remains today is the house, which stands beside the old A11 road.

TAVERHAM MILL, c. 1904

Taverham Mill was in existence before 1850. During the 19th century, it operated as a paper mill and produced top quality paper for bank notes, bibles and 'The Times' newspaper.

The mill ceased production in 1901 and was demolished later in 1920. All that remains now is the old canteen.

THE SALVATION ARMY, c. 1914

Members of the Salvation Army photographed prior to collecting money for their appeal during the Salvation Army Self-Denial Week.

The horse and cart were loaned by G.W. Lambert, fruit and vegetable grower, of Lakenham.

SALVATION ARMY OUTING, c. 1912

Members of the Norwich Salvation Army photographed in Ber Street on the occasion of their annual outing.
The two horse and carts, which belonged to the Norwich Co-operative Society, are seen passing the 'George IV' public
house (72, Ber Street) and the entrance to the yard at the rear of the 'George IV'.
The Salvation Army barracks were located at 48, Ber Street.

The Coronation Bonfire on St. James' Hill, Norwich. The Gift of the Lord Mayor. 30 Ft. High, 20 Ft. Diameter at Base. June 22nd 1911.

CORONATION BONFIRE, 1911

In celebration of the Coronation of H.M. King George V in 1911, many giant bonfires were built forming a national bonfire chain all over the country.

Norwich constructed its Coronation Bonfire on St. James' Hill, Mousehold Heath. It was 80 ft high and 20 ft diameter at its base.

At 11 p.m. on 22nd June, 1911, fifty rockets were ignited and rose to form a Coronation bouquet. This display was then followed by the playing of the National Anthem.

TANK WEEK, c. 1918

Tank Week was held to promote the sale of War Bonds. The tank was transported to Norwich by rail from London, and parked in front of the Guildhall in Market Place. Its attraction resulted in a total sum of over one million pounds to be contributed during the week; Norwich being one of thirty-three cities achieving one million pounds.
Tanks, similar to the one illustrated, were first used during the Somme Offensive on 15th September, 1916. During the summer of 1916, the tank crews were trained in a vast secret enclosure near Thetford.

MR. B.C. HUCKS, THE 'DAILY MAIL' AIRMAN AT NORWICH. AUG. 1912.

THE 'DAILY MAIL' AIRMAN AT NORWICH, 1912

During 1912, the 'Daily Mail' monoplane, 'Firefly', flew on a promotional tour around the country.
The 70 h.p. Blériot monoplane, piloted by Mr. Bentfield C. Hucks, arrived in Norwich on 3rd August, 1912. It was the first aeroplane to fly over Norwich on its journey from Crowhurst Farm, Gorleston to Church Lane, Eaton.

NORWICH CITY FOOTBALL CLUB, 1908

Norwich City Football Club was formed in 1902. In 1908, Norwich City moved from their original ground on Newmarket Road to 'The Nest' on Rosary Road.

This card shows the ground, built in a disused chalk pit, under construction. A fifty foot high concrete wall was required to retain the cliff in the background. The first match at the ground resulted in a 2–1 win for the Canaries against Fulham in a friendly match on 1st September, 1908. 'The Nest' is now an industrial estate; one of the occupiers being the book wholesalers, Bertram Books Ltd.

NORWICH CITY FOOTBALL CLUB. Season 1908-9.

A. Turner   J. C. Nutchey   J. W. Howes   J. Pyke   M. Nattrass   A. E. Barham   W. T. Blyth
(Asst. Manager)   *(Referee)*   *(Hon. Sec. & D.)*   *(Chairman)*   *(Director)*   *(Director)*   *(Director)*

Newlands, Long, G. Martin, C. Greenfield, Tomlinson, Wagstaffe, G. Porter, Roney, Beale, McQueen *(Trainer)*

Livingstone   Coxhead   McEwen *(Capt.)*   Flanagan   Whiteman   Allsopp

Church   Smith   Silor   Pegg

NORWICH CITY FOOTBALL CLUB, 1908–9

This team group depicts the fine body of men to represent Norwich City during their first season at 'The Nest'.
Norwich City competed in the Southern League, finishing an undistinguished third from bottom.
The low point of the season was a record 10–2 defeat at Swindon, while the highlight must have been the 1–0 F.A. Cup
win over Liverpool who were in the First Division.

THE NORWICH BELLMAN & HIS DOG PRINCE.   COPYRIGHT

THE NORWICH BELLMAN, c. 1906

This postcard shows the last Norwich Bellman, Harry Moulton, and his dog Prince. He is standing in front of the Dolphin Inn, Heigham Street. Harry served as Bellman from 1905 until this office was abolished. Notice the dog with documents in his mouth.

This traditional post was resumed in 1986 when David Bullock was officially appointed Bellman/Town Crier.

DRAYTON POST OFFICE, p.u. 1917

Mr Smith, sub-postmaster, with his family photographed outside Drayton sub-post office.

The Notice board reads, 'Post Office for money orders, parcel post, savings bank, telegraph, and express delivery business'.

Notice the postman with his delivery tricycle in the foreground.

4685 EATON BAKERY.

EATON STREET, c. 1906

Looking towards Cringleford and showing Eaton Street with the junction with Church Lane on the left. Eaton Bakery is now occupied by a newsagent. Further down Eaton Street, the cottages are now shops, and in the centre, is the 'Red Lion' public house, built in the late 17th century.
On the right is Eaton Post Office, and the taller building to the left has now been demolished.

COLNEY POST OFFICE, p.u. 1906

Colney Post Office was situated on the Watton road. The single storey building to the left was occupied by a blacksmith's forge.

Both buildings are now occupied as private houses and are near the BUPA Hospital.

NORWICH UNION INSURANCE SOCIETIES, 1937

An unusual advertising postcard published by the Norwich Union Insurance Societies to commemorate the Coronation of H.M. King George VI in 1937.

THE GREAT TONIC RESTORATIVE.—SOUVENIR FRANCO-BRITISH EXHIBITION, 1908.

With the Compliments of COLEMAN & Co., Ltd., Wincarnis Works, NORWICH.

STANDS HIGHEST IN PUBLIC OPINION

COLEMANS
WINCARNIS
COLEMAN'S
Wincarnis

MARKET PLACE, NORWICH.

RECOMMENDED BY THOUSANDS OF THE MEDICAL PROFESSION. OVER 8,000 TESTIMONIALS RECEIVED.

COLEMAN'S ADVERTISING POSTCARD, c. 1908

An attractive give-away advertising postcard produced by Coleman & Co. Ltd., Wincarnis Works, Norwich, as a souvenir for the Franco-British Exhibition held in London in 1908

The postcard view shows Market Place at the turn of the century. The bottle of Wincarnis was hand-tinted in colour for special effect.

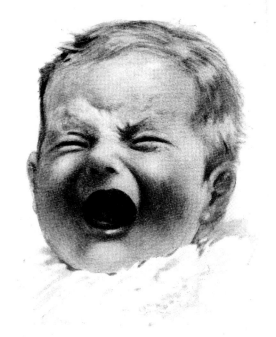

Open all
night at
NORWICH.

This comic postcard was published by Wilt and Kray of London. Postcards of this type were published in vast quantities and over-printed to order with the name of any town or village throughout the country.